Whether touching on brutal history of the American demagogue, a "torch of purple lilacs," or the poet's "last look" at his deceased beloved, the vision of John Krumberger's *When I Was a King* is both piercing and large-souled. This is poetry in the service of living, responsive to whatever experience brings. The pages move through profound personal grief, "this wind/ that blows through me as if I am an emptiness," yet remain stubbornly open to the solace and sustenance of memory, attention, kindness, love, awe, joy that "rises up surprising and immense." Krumberger's honesty and generosity turn the reader into fellow traveler and gatherer of meanings: "And so, write them/ in the book, the names, the mysteries,/ we owe them at least that." The deep humanity of this book will break you open and remind you why poetry matters.

JAY UDALL
author of *Because a Fire in Our Heads*

"Poetry begins with generosity," insists John Krumberger, and in poems that have as their backdrop both current politics and the death of his wife—"what is this wind/ that blows through me as if I am an emptiness?"—the poet moves beyond anger and resignation toward simple pleasures, imagining how "grass feels/ receiving the touch of rain" or seeing his daughter approaching in a crowded city, "flowing there/ along that radiant river of faces." Yes. *When I Was a King* is filled with such moments, striking its variations on our daily affirmations, its poems always burgeoning: "You remember a phrase, then a whole song from the old language." Apricity. That obsolete word meaning the warmth of the sun in winter. That's the word that comes to mind while reading this moving collection.

MICHAEL WATERS
author of *Celestial Joyride*

John Krumberger's *When I Was a King* delivers a calm testimony to paying attention. There are jests and surprises and the markings of memory, loss, and beauty. These are deeply felt poems crafted with passion and commitment to "finding gold, dark stories." He offers radiant and truthful portrayals of the small-town America where he grew up and reflections on the challenging America of current times. These are poems of family, place, and spirit. And the reader understands just how much he knows in "the way poetry begins with generosity." A beautiful book of rememberings and beginnings.

DIANE JARVENPA
author of *Shy Lands*

WHEN I WAS A KING

John Krumberger

Fernwood
PRESS

When I Was a King

©2025 by John Krumberger

Fernwood Press
Newberg, Oregon
www.fernwoodpress.com

All rights reserved. No part may be reproduced
for any commercial purpose by any method without
permission in writing from the copyright holder.

Printed in the United States of America

Cover and page design: Mareesa Fawver Moss
Cover art: Aaron Blanco Tejedor via Unsplash
Author photo: Glenn Hirsch

ISBN 978-1-59498-159-3

In Memory of Cris Higgin

*Once for each thing. Just once,
no more. And never again. But
to have been
this once completely, even if
only once:
to have been with the
earth, seems beyond undoing.*

      (From Rainer Maria Rilke's
  "Ninth Elegy" from Duino Elegies)

CONTENTS

Acknowledgments 11
I 13
    When I Was a King 14
    Gardener 15
    Praise Song for Feet 16
    South Side 18
    First Death 19
    A Free Man 20
    Paper Route 21
    Copycat Music 23
    Wisconsin Supper Club 25
    Elysium 26
    New York City Poem for Emily 27
    Beer 28
    Election Day, November 2016 30
    Kickapoo, Most Crooked of Rivers 31
    First Summer of the Trump Presidency 32

II 33
    Crazy Love 34
    The Wrestlers 35

Cass Lake 37
Downtown Minneapolis 38
Here 39
Solitudes 40
The Dancers 44
Proletarian Poet 45
An Accounting 46
Advent 47
First Session 48
East of the Cheyenne Reservation 49
The Parlor 50

III 51
This Is It 52
Ash 55
Why We Still Write Poems as the
    Country Succumbs to Meanness 56
A Dream in Black and White 57
The Heart 58
Last Look 59
My Garden Now 61
This Moment 62
Uncovering the Roses 63
Autumn Comes to
    the North Shore 64
These Days 65

IV 67
Pilgrimage, Blackhawk Island 68
Ordinary Time, Jefferson, Iowa 69
Bicycling as a Form of Prayer 70
Dirt 71
Birthday 72
Rosary Society, St. Mary's Church,
    Racine, Wisconsin 73
Poem for the Dog Jaya 74

19 Wadham Gardens..75
Days of Bees and Indigo...76
What To Do in New York City.................................77
This..79
October Journal...80

Notes on the Poems..85
Title Index...87
First Line Index..91

ACKNOWLEDGMENTS

Some of these poems were first published in the following journals: *Abandoned Mine:* "These Days"; *Blue Mountain Review:* "Pilgrimage Black Hawk Island"; *Bryant Literary Review:* "Copy Cat Music"; *Caesura:* "Downtown Minneapolis," "Here"; *Cave Wall:* "This Is It"; *Claudius Speaks:* "The Gardener"; *Coal City Review:* "19 Wadham Gardens"; *Comstock Review:* "Birthday"; *Connecticut River Review:* "First Summer of the Trump Presidency"; *Flint Hills Review:* "East of the Cheyenne Reservation"; *Front Range Review:* "The Dancers"; *Gris Gris:* "An Accounting," "Solitudes," "The Heart"; *Hospital Drive:* "First Session"; *Last Stanza Journal:* "Elysium"; *Main Street Rag:* "New York City Poem for Emily"; *Midwest Review:* "Proletarian Poet"; *Muddy River Review:* "This"; *Mudfish:* "Beer", "South Side"; *Naugatuck Review:* "Paper Route"; *Nine Muses:* "Election Day 2016," "A Dream in Black and White"; *Plainsong:* "Poem for the Dog Jaya"; *Red River Review:* "Days of Bees and Indigo"; *Salt Poetry Journal:* "Crazy Love"; *Sangam:* "Ash," "The Parlor," "When I Was a King," "Rosary Society, St. Mary's Church, Racine Wisconsin"; *Slab;* "Bicycling as a Form of Prayer"; *Southern Poetry Review:* "A Free Man"; *Steam Ticket* "First Death"; *The Stillwater Review:* "Kickapoo, Most Crooked of Rivers"; *Switched on Gutenberg:* "Advent"; *Talking*

River Review: "Praise Song for Feet," "The Wrestlers"; *Talking Stick: "Dirt"*; *Third Wednesday*: "Why We Still Write Poems as the Country Succumbs to Meanness," "Ordinary Time"; *Unbroken*: "Cass Lake"; *Visions International*: "What To Do in New York City"

"The Dancers" was reprinted in *Ocotillo Review* with credit acknowledged to the *Front Range Review and* included in *Allegro and Adagio II: Poems on Dance,* Johnny Tucker editor, Imagination Press, 2018.

"Beer" was included in *Last Call: The Anthology of Beer, Wine and Spirits Poetry* edited by James Bertolino, World Enough Writers, 2018.

"The Heart" was included in *It Starts With Hope: Writing of Hope Donated to the Center For Victims of Torture, Minneapolis MN,* edited by Ted Bowman and Betsy Brown, 2016.

"This Moment" was included in *A 21st Century Plague: Poetry from a Pandemic* edited by Elayne Clift, University Professors Press, 2021.

"Bicycling as a Form of Prayer" was included in the 2023 Wisconsin Poetry Calendar.

I am indebted to Howie Faestein, Roberta Feins, Susan Sailer, Janet Barry, Emily Krumberger, and Thomas R. Smith for their invaluable help with the poems in this book.

I

WHEN I WAS A KING

Because I was a king
no moon could adjudicate me.
I'd hide wherever I pleased,
wild-eyed, ready to pounce,
and they thrilled to it,

mother and daughter
chirping with excitement
as they rounded the curve,
daughter calling
Papa, where are you?

while I waited submerged
in withered October leaves,
having practiced my falling
dead impersonation
for just such a chance,

the galaxy expanding
as I held my breath,
listening for footsteps,
back when the world loved us,
and we loved each other without fault.

GARDENER

I watch her on her knees
fingering the loam
where slithering crepuscular creatures
scurry back to their tunneled homes.
The open earth no longer at rest,
a new year begins here in May,
bluebells waiting in pots
as she whispers something
—*what is it?*—
then lays them in their holes.

Bonemeal and ash,
her voice a torch
for the darkness they enter,
spiraling down to bind the worlds
above and below,
and she doesn't see me watching her
talking to the rabbit,
explaining it all,
then tilting as she walks,
perfectly happy with her bucket of dirt.

PRAISE SONG FOR FEET

Some of us still snuggle
a pet blanket at night,
flannel tucked up to chin
until the comforted mind
clicks like a lock.
Others safely nod off
only with a loaded gun
under their pillow—
keeping its steely eye open
so that its owner's eyes can shut.

Still others noodle
on cell phones for hours
recalling the old Three Stooges
nonsensical dictum
wake up and go to sleep.
While some souls enter their beds
raucously uncalmed,
night a café with nothing
but insomnia on its menu.

For me my feet brushing each other
with the slightest skin
to skin contact does the trick,
whispering to each other
such soft endearments
as *sweetie* and *honey*
as I close my eyes.

Just the slightest skin contact
though enough to remember
that I live in a body.
We are like the changing grass,
says the psalm
that monks sing at night.
Imagine how that grass feels
receiving the touch of rain.

SOUTH SIDE

> *Whatever can come to a city can come to this city.*
> *Under the tall compulsion*
>   *of the past*
> *I see the city*
>   *change like a man changing*
>   —Muriel Rukeyser

Eva dying in the apartment facing the alley.
Grace who pretends to be her roommate,
beside herself.
The paramedics stiffening: one two three lift.
The last decade of the factories
before Reagan's war on the unions.
Each moment an ice floe slowly melting.
Sunday shouts and singing
lifted from Calvary Baptist Ministries.
The morning sun on unmade beds
or basketball hoops clamped to wooden boards
hanging above garages in the alley,
the same alley between Franklin and Center
that reappears in dreams.
Now the block like a mouth missing half its teeth,
the city absorbing each loss
until its body is slowed by it.

FIRST DEATH

The not so ironically surnamed
son of the owner
of Solomon's Standard gas station—
he possessed of the same large hands
and slow wit as Lenny
from *Of Mice and Men*—
comforts the still-drunk man,
sobbing *a child, a child*,
and indeed, a small boy's boots appear
from beneath the man's car parked
in the street as police arrive
walking silently like figures in a dream—
enormous August clouds peering down,
while something surges through my chest
like lightning or God
or maybe the spirit of the boy.

A FREE MAN

Summer, the college town half full, maybe less,
and the rented house empty of roommates.
I'm learning the night language of birds and chimes,
and in this schoolyard afternoon,
teaching myself tennis, working a sweat
as I slam the ball against a wall,
then sprint to return the rebound,
sometimes squarely, often not.

Recent graduate without prospects,
rank, or trade, not on my way anywhere,
a free man, alone, afraid
of being alone and also craving it.
The ball careens in every direction,
my opponent winning the game
though I don't care. There's no score to keep.

PAPER ROUTE

Walking up and down stairs,
behind and alongside houses
that no longer exist—
two years I plodded those blocks,
day after day
now razed and replaced
by grass and flowered walks
that girdle the corporate offices
of Johnson Wax on Franklin Street
where Stephanie Petz once
sunbathed in a bikini
on a narrow strip of grass,
her boyfriend glaring,
his knife whittling a root
while I passed quickly as I could,
to toss a rolled-up paper
onto the sunken, slumping porch.

And where is Mrs. Hill,
who Saturday morning, robe open,
paid her sixty cents?
Where the bachelor apartments
with their frying smells, unmade beds,
cigarette clouds escaping
through a slit of dark
in the middle of the day?
Snake grass sprawled along the tracks
where Solomon's Standard station
bordered 14th street
at the end of the route.
Donna Rodriguez, one year ahead of me
in school, dropped out

to have her baby boy
who would be past fifty now.
Next door Mrs. Dalminiak
counted pennies from a jar
as the sun rose in her village in Poland.
Last night in a dream
I waited in that modest, widowed house,
as resplendent light revealed rooms
passing into other rooms
each one more regal.
Then in the way in a dream
anything is possible
I heard the scripture verse:
In my father's house are many mansions.

COPYCAT MUSIC

I never asked his name—
no suitable pause between
the torrent of New-York-accented syllables
flowing from that lovely
Italian-Portuguese mouth
dragging on cigarette after cigarette
or erupting into spasms
of an indrawn, cardiac-sounding laugh—
though I marveled at the happenstance
of such a near exotic creature
surfacing in Racine, wedged
between the Danish bakery
and the Walgreens pharmacy.

Copy Cat Music featured rock, punk,
hip hop, soul, R and B, and anything
and everything from the '60s.
An act of love to preserve
the ache and ecstasy of the time,
though not in candled, incensed fashion,
just row after unscented row
of vinyl and wall posters:
Hendrix, Joplin, Donna Summer,
the menace of the python
sleeping in its cage,
a gumball machine, juke box,
fish tank, old and new turntables,
a Gibson guitar for sale,
dance music playing.

And whoever he was,
he was a match
lit in the rain, maybe six years
then gone, without warning,
not enough fellow oddballs I guess
to support and care for the cat—
those few dwindling souls
who still believe
that music can change the world,
now more alone
as silence encroaches upon their lives.

WISCONSIN SUPPER CLUB

The locals share a body type—
strong, thick, heavy, hairy—
and a wildness with the animals.

The young man's shirt proclaiming
"Lions Not Lambs,"
American flag emblazoned on the back,

recalls how the bear stared insolently
at us as if to say
you're the interlopers here.

A dark foreboding road, off the grid,
potholes, poplars, white pine, spruce,
no turnarounds, our devices failing,

yet now we're settled in to fried fish,
French fries, coleslaw, beer,
an all-you-can-eat bacchanalia,

words blurred to one communal eating sound,
the lake outside bejeweled by forest,
the forest bejeweled by sunset

as the platters at each table
are slowly winnowed down,
only to be replenished by more.

ELYSIUM

And after the rain there was bird song, and we drove through a place of lakes and forests called Elysium or maybe Wisconsin, and because it was early summer, darkness had not arrived, just the endless mystery of twilight, dreams biding their time, lady slipper in bloom, deer curled up in an open field, or curled up into the soft bed of a ravine, all color fused into the gauziness that precedes nightfall, and if we were sinking into a dark well, we let ourselves go deeper. Then finally the moon rose as a ripe strawberry and God spoke an eloquent silence, and by some trick of shadow and night, the trees appeared to be walking, and the mosquitos hunted us, and a lifetime passed and then another, strawberry, beams lighting the grass until I knew for certain I had traveled there before.

NEW YORK CITY POEM FOR EMILY

As August light slanted golden on the leaves
it almost killed me to know we would lose you
to that mildewed, diaphanous city
and that bastard Frank O'Hara talking about the moon
gliding broken-faced over bridges, lose you
to that dark angel Roy and his Jazz Passengers,
Roy, who once claimed that nature made him nervous—
crossing into Manhattan, he had swept his hand
out the car window, waving to water, sky,
girders, suspensions, harbors, and pigeons,
while screaming *this, this is nature*—nevertheless,
when I spotted you at 10th and Broadway,
dressed in your multi-colored shift,
a little unsure of yourself and tilting
slightly toward the adult world,
I thought *butterfly, butterfly, lighter than air*,
though I indulged my image only a moment,
knowing it wasn't time for yesterday's artifice,
not as faces came up from the underground,
the sky a vast savannah full of fierce animal clouds
disassembling into smaller animals
skittering away until the sun broke free,
and I had to squint to even see you flowing there
along that radiant river of faces.

BEER

Who knows where my father
found a lifetime of watered down
discount labels, butt of countless jokes
from his progeny as we grew older
and fancied ourselves knowledgeable
about choices in the world.

Now I have a daughter in her twenties
who considers me out of step,
and maybe I am.
Every January, she joins me
to visit his grave,
stopping first at a liquor store,
trying to be subtle
since you can't just ask
for the worst can of beer in the place.

This year we bought him an Old Style
then drove through a snow squall
that lit up the sky on a country road
bound for Holy Family Cemetery.
Neither of us wore boots,
striding the dark winter meadow
past gravestones, guided by the light
of her cell phone,
she, placing the beer in front of him,
then stepping aside to allow me time
to tell him about the year.

Just then I looked up
to something flashing
in the fogged darkness,
both of us afraid to walk toward it
though we did—in that little city
full of so many of my people—
discovering blue Christmas lights
hooked to a generator,
then draped over a grave
that drawing closer we found belonged
to my cousin, Mary Bodi.

I never knew her
except in childhood,
yet there she was, and there I was
with my own child
still puzzling out this world,
surprised at how happy I was
to receive the dead
with their jests and surprises.

ELECTION DAY, NOVEMBER 2016

(In memory of my mother)

Three days after we buried her
the weather abruptly changed,
and I failed to wear the proper shoes
for rain freezing into snow.
How I wanted to say *the worst is over now*—
nursing home, feeding tube,
her bruised arms and legs,
the thrush in her mouth done with and gone—
but the cold front would have contradicted me:
first a constant drip from roofs
and trees rivering the gutters,
then the sneer of ice with its ugly grin
on puddles lit by street lamps,
finally, the drifts seeping into my wingtips,
never to be the same again.
Once the feet are cold, the body follows.
Shivering I recalled my James Joyce:
the snow *general* falling over
the dazed, *mutinous* country.

KICKAPOO, MOST CROOKED OF RIVERS

Kickapoo—one who goes here and then there (Algonquin)

One who goes here and then there.
One hundred thirty miles to traverse sixty miles
from Wildcat Mountain to Wauzeka, where
it empties into the Wisconsin, the Mississippi, the Gulf.

One hundred thirty miles to traverse sixty miles,
here then there, past hills unawakened from sleep,
it empties into the Wisconsin, the Mississippi, the Gulf,
sun-glinted riffles rounding the bend, gone.

Here then there, past hills unawakened from sleep,
dreams of the Sauk, the Meswakis, the Fox.
Sun-glinted riffles rounding the bend, gone,
ghost mist erasing the bluffs.

Dreams of the Sauk, the Meswakis, the Fox,
murdered, starved, resettled here then there,
ghost mist erasing the bluffs,
and voices heard speaking in tongues.

Murdered, starved, resettled here then there,
surviving in the names of towns
and voices heard speaking in tongues,
in near words, in almost rememberings.

Surviving in the names of towns,
in the no sound of rain,
in near words, in almost rememberings.
One who goes here and then there.

FIRST SUMMER OF THE TRUMP PRESIDENCY

Something askew in the universe now:
two once-in-a-hundred-year storms
and wasps attacking without provocation.
So what good is her belief in fair play, her love of beauty,
when stung by such hatefulness she can hardly breathe?
Her tongue swells as she lurches through the garden,
trying to recall the counsel of Marcus Aurelius:
a calm mind in the face of injustice or pain.

In the park across from the hospital,
young men play basketball as twilight extends to evening.
It could be a painting: softening liquid sky,
athletes suspended in air, a ball bouncing against pavement,
repeating the rhythm of ordinary life
as if nothing has changed.

II

CRAZY LOVE

As a hunter's moon stalks the streets of old northeast
a man slow dances with his wife at the Weasel Club,
kitchen about to close, some slapdash trio finishing their set,

their pot-bellied, T-shirted, sweet-voiced front man
crooning Van Morrison while shuffling side to side,
making love to a microphone,

he one of those angels dissatisfied
with an eternity of watching, who longs for coffee
or for heartache, thinking them more pure.

Eleven dead in a synagogue in Pittsburgh,
pipe bombs proliferating in the mail,
sociopath in the White House green-lighting it all.

The grizzled bass guitar player fingering his chords
bows his head the way the faithful bowed in prayer
before the gunman opened fire.

Now the angel is singing about love, love, love, crazy love,
while the man, his wife, the cook, drinkers at the bar
and the waitress (who is not ready yet to give up on men)
receive the notes, placing them inside their shirts, inside their
blouses.

For an hour they are more kind.

As if kindness could speak saying *I will change you,
make you better.*

THE WRESTLERS

Today I wrestled the devil anxiety,
      fought him to a draw
           which means
the match resumes tomorrow.
He used illegal holds
      and struck below the belt,
the day's heat pressing down
      on us both,
           more harsh
than my most severe recriminations.

      Nevertheless
after it passed
      I was left not wrecked,
           but more like a man
with a winning ticket
      in his hand,

the wind dispersing bougainvillea scent
      while God played guitar
           on the beach,
singing romantic ballads
      so sweetly
that I forgot about the morning,

or rather I reconsidered it,
      thinking not a devil at all
but death taking my account,
      sizing me up
the way wrestlers often do.

And as the wind was a second wind for me,
    I could breathe again deeply,
acquiring in the act
    a brotherly sentiment
toward my opponent.

And how could I feel otherwise
    toward something that had held me
        so closely,
            so intimately?

CASS LAKE

Some winter days the sheen off the lake can be blinding, white pines along shore bending forward like old men looking at their shoes. Two miles into town the dialysis clinic, closed on Sunday, dozes under rags of dirty clouds. When the wind blows hard it obliterates the only road, leaving icehouses stranded out there. Maybe it's too late to change the way you live, your stomach sour again, the drifts piling up onto the highway. The few scraggly windbreak trees like the last hairs on a bald man's head aren't enough to stop anything from happening. Still, when you breathe the cold air something settles and softens. The walleye filets are thawing in the kitchen, a recipe for tartar sauce scribbled on a torn scrap of paper. You remember a phrase, then a whole song from the old language.

DOWNTOWN MINNEAPOLIS

Whatever is going to happen has already happened—that's the vibe these streets exude. At one end, the Hennepin Avenue bridge stretches out wide like the saint who kept his arms open day and night so that a sparrow could nest in his palms. And the bridge glitters. Still, it's no use. You can feel it just a few blocks in, how the off-duty buildings slump, depressed, anorexic, silently angry, while busses burrow deeper into the night hours, driverless and without passengers.

It's always the same question—*how did I get here?*—asked to avoid the other questions. Look down the nearly deserted canyon in the shadow of the towers, and you'll find that no one stops or strolls, though a few of the dead hunch against the wind-blown snow.

Scraps of paper, neon lights, tawdry sin parlors. A door opens, and a face appears like a newborn pushed out from a womb. A line of figures resembling tall insects advance across the parking lot terrain. The mind stops using language. You can't feel or imagine the suffering of these buildings, or maybe it's a perfect act of empathy, the way you've turned to stone.

HERE

Here the invisible gremlins which hover around us have swooped upon the weakest of them, tearing out what used to be called personality. A man growls "fucking asshole" at whoever speaks to him. A woman weeps and weeps. Another wanders into each room, the aides finding her there searching for home. Human odors mix brazenly with flowery drawings on the wall. Has anyone recently seen the sky? When they touch themselves, can they summon the torrents that once seized them? Here downstream, in this brackish torpor, gravity pushes down so hard it's crushing them.

SOLITUDES

I

In Amsterdam a poet is hired to attend the funerals where no one else comes, offering a poem for the unmourned:

immigrants, drug mules, sex workers, lonely tourists, the forgotten old, their footprints erased, no trace of how they arrived.

Farewell sir,
without papers, without identity. What were you looking for?
How much did you lose along the way?

II

From the insular world of the car, I watched ghosts and goblins complete their trick or treat rounds in each town I passed while I plunged deeper into the Driftless Region on my way to a cloistered silence I thought I would live for

though the holy atheists, Keats and Camus, claimed me instead. The character Tarrou in Camus's *The Plague* reveals to the doctor his desire to be a saint who doesn't believe in God. At the very end Camus warns, "the plague bacillus never dies or disappears." And now it has returned, this time in our country.

III

After the prophet's time in the desert his daily bread tasted like
ashes in his mouth, and flowing water dried to dust on his skin.
He seemed to hate comfort even more than the worship of false
gods, his eyes remaining open the rest of his life, resisting the
sleep of ordinary contentment.

*Ye have built houses of hewn stone, but shall not dwell in them,
have planted pleasant vineyards but shall not drink wine of them.
The day of Yahweh is a day of darkness and not a day of light—*
or some such sentiment as he pressed a burning coal flush to
blistered lips.

IV

The green heart of summer: wild buttercups, delphinium,
Virginia bluebells, black-eyed Susan, a cloud of gnats, the deer
studying me as slowly I bicycle to the top of the bluff

or the register at the summit of Glacier Peak, an icy wind
taunting our triumph. An embossed photo of a six-year-old boy
next to where climbers sign their names. What was his story?
Lonely sentinel exposed to every kind of weather,

or the photograph of my father, his foot raised onto the running
board of a Packard town car, the victorious country hurtling
toward the new decade-steel of new buildings, asphalt of new
highways poured for suburbs rinsed of history and burnished
with convenience? He squints into the afternoon; white T-shirt,
black hair, muscular physique, all saying Brando, though already
the flashbacks begin to haunt his dreams.

V

He thinks I am asleep and stands in the dim hall touching himself. I hear from the bath piss streaming into the bowl. He has come back to us, half-moons recessed on his forehead where electrodes were attached. The jagged current taught him to forget, so he wanders each room, the house breathing in, breathing out.

VI

Burying the rabbit Sweet Pea in the yard. *I bequeath myself to the dirt, to grow from the grass I love.* How did she survive the night we accidentally left her out alone, waiting at the side-porch door patient and forgiving as a Buddhist? Now the transient arc of contentment curves toward an uncertain dark she'll have to travel.

VII

Each time life feels too much to bear, a kindness visits me, and I feel totally loved. Margie wrote the words in a spiral notebook that Glenn found a year after her death. Better at dying than living, she found courage and purpose she couldn't find in the world. At their 25th anniversary, a kind of farewell gathering, she played Chopin's spirit-infused Prelude Number 4, her face radiant, the notes lingering, the way beauty touches us for a moment and then is gone. Chopin, sick most of his life, once said, "My body is a disappointment to me. I pretend it doesn't exist."

VIII

Before his suicide the man splurged for a gourmet meal at
the restaurant adjacent to the theater. He finished a bottle of
Sauvignon alone, drove to the Mississippi, filling his pockets
with rocks like Virginia Woolf, then stepped in current,
disappearing into dark waters downstream. The waiter
remembered his quiet voice and the tip beyond generous.
His sister remembers his gentleness, brilliance, and vulnerability.
She feared for more than twenty years the call she finally
received. "I don't belong here," he once said. How is it she knew
even then he was referring not to that crowd, that room, or even
their family, but rather to the world.

IX

Did the sight of olive trees outside the asylum press further upon
Van Gogh
        or touch him from beyond this world?
Clearly, those gnarled limbs reach up to something in his yellow
pulsating sky.
We are all ground between the millstones to become bread, he wrote
his brother Theo. *Even face to face with an illness that breaks me up
and frightens me, this belief remains unshaken.*

THE DANCERS

> *isn't there still something singing?*
> —Ada Limon

The poem asks
whether there's still something singing.
And since I repeat the question,
you can tell I believe there is,
but then who listens anyhow?

She does,
and where has it gotten her?
Two years out of college
living with her parents
saddled with debt
we pay her and her dance troupe
to listen for us;

theater snow falling around the stage
as he lifts her,
somehow summoning the strength
though he's hardly eaten for days,
the company worried
since he's broken up with his boyfriend,

both he and she pivoting
to complete their rendezvous,
then leaping to a glimmered sky
that holds them like stars,
his head resting on her breast,
unaware, transfixed,
both of them listening.

PROLETARIAN POET

—for Lyle Daggett 1954-2018

At an early '90s memorial for Thomas McGrath;
when musicians struck up The Internationale,
you sang, arm raised in salute,
other hand over your heart,
while I half-stood, half-sat, embarrassed
at not knowing the words.

Now I raise my arm to salute you
who kept clear of fashions,
literary or otherwise,
handing out pamphlets on street corners,
wage slogging away for thirty years at AT&T,
riding the 21A down Lake Street,
always keeping your flame alive
regardless of sore hip, shortness of breath,
knowing your truth, trusting it.

And alone at night
you'd enjoy your view
of the Pioneers and Old Soldiers Cemetery.
No wife, no car, no portfolio,
at peace with one last joke to spare,
dying on Christmas, most holy day
of the consumer liturgical year,
perfect and unfinished
as any honest poem.

AN ACCOUNTING

And for your crimes against humanity, Mr. Trump,
you are sentenced by the Heavenly Court
to an incarnation in Racine, Wisconsin,
only this time your father will not be a mogul
but rather a man-child unsheltered by those streets.
And you shall wander the alleys between Franklin
and Center, lowering your eyes before the police.
And your anger will not be rewarded.
And you will cast far and wide for your daily bread,
cleaning the balky toilets at old Dana Hall,
where George Wallace spoke in 1972, testifying
to his audience that Washington politicians carried
peanut butter sandwiches in their fancy briefcases,
that they were pussy-footing on bussing, and pussy-footing

on welfare, while the crowd howled like a pack of excited dogs,
for he was a demagogue, skilled as yourself, and in a photograph
from *The Journal Times* one sees the leering face
of Arthur Bremer there stalking his prey, waiting
with the bullet that would shatter Mr. Wallace's spine
later that month, purifying him with unending pain,
until slowly he became a human being needing to meet
with the ministers of Montgomery to apologize before he died.
All of this is written. Our days are like the changing grass.
Nevertheless, the mercy of this court demands that it show
no mercy not proportionate with the just and the right.
Therefore, you are to be cursed with servitude, afflicted
with want, a hungry ghost, cold and without comfort
until a time deemed suitable for your release.

ADVENT

> *In those days there was no king in Israel.*
> *Everyone did what was right in his own eyes.*
> —Judges 21:25

In those days when there was no king
in the land, and every person did
what was right in their own eyes,
hope warmed itself over the fires
outside the tents,
outside the fourth precinct station—
another son's skull rent unto death,
and channel 5 crafting its story
in the newsroom first,
then driving to the site
to interview the police union chief,
fanning his own flames—
and it was witnessed:
the son handcuffed,
unarmed when shot,
the people assembled, waiting for truth,
days without comfort, days without rule,
when every man did what was right
in his own eyes.

FIRST SESSION

> *The therapist is always a mother.*
> —Sigmund Freud

At the doorway introduction
his eyes, hands, and body
say *you won't know me,*
then his voice adds:
"My sponsor says I should talk to you,"
which translates as: *it's not my idea*
and *you won't know me*
and *I've come now you do the rest.*

                    Yet,
here in this place where I preside,
balding and maternal,
silence secures the space between us
until my reassuring voice arrives
commanding him to his chair

where memory is smoothed to a stone
suddenly found in his pocket,
his story seeping out
from an underground spring,
the poetry of it surprising him,

his tears ceasing to scare him
as he slowly discards his mask,
and I see the boy
who wants forgiveness,
see sun breaking
through morning fog
while I adjust my own mask,
moving closer with my chair.

EAST OF THE CHEYENNE RESERVATION

There where the Missouri surges
treacherous as a whirlpool,
a boy steps into the current,
stripped to his shorts,
cold water caressing his thighs,
his arms a machine
cutting the water into swaths.

Later awakening in a cheap hotel
he wonders where he's been:
two ex-wives, two daughters
living in another state.
He pours his booze
down a rat-hole sink,
watching the stream escape

while outside hay bales lay like boulders
deposited on the grass
and geese glide south in formation
tight as the M-22s he once flew.

Nowhere in all the miles of empty space
to flee from himself.

THE PARLOR

> *It is only after it is liberated in analysis*
> *that the self begins to be articulate.*
> —Alice Miller

They come to this parlor of alchemy
a little afraid of hope, yet they hope.

Music flares from the bistro downstairs,
like a soundtrack to the mystery

of what we do here. And it's an honor
truly to prospect beside them,

finding the core, finding the gold,
the stories dark, sometimes for months,

with shards of memory much too heavy
for anyone to bear alone,

each impurity unraveling,
molecules breaking down,

shame transformed to grief
then energy and soul until one day

as light streams through my east-facing windows,
I see we are all made of it

and wonder who has shined
for me the way I do for them.

III

THIS IS IT

You bring *The New York Times* with you
which you won't get to read.
We careen down the Franklin hill
to cross the Mississippi,
joined by my twenty-two-year-old self
who has traversed a different bridge
to a new life, a new state,
exclaiming: *This is it.*
We welcome him, welcome the musicians
he lived with that autumn,
they who jammed all night and slept all day
while he bicycled to the university.

Our latitude is 44.973 north,
longitude 93.258 west, zip code 55414.
The leaves along shore luxuriate
in the August light, the same leaves
that were not leaves easily
on your birthday in the spring,
buds pushing, fighting to exist
as you coughed with what we thought was asthma.

There's room enough for your roses
and the cardinal pair who nested in our garden,
room for your garden, for your paintings,
for the rabbits Sweet Pea and Lulu,
room for *Sherlock Holmes* and *Downton Abbey*—
all crammed into my Honda Civic.

Your younger self is here
smiling as she answers the door
on the Tuesday of our first date,
sizing me up and having the advantage

because she is so pretty—
and your bearing down birthing self,
calling my name though our noses touch,
and your silly nun-costumed
Halloween-self, flirting
with my vampire-self.

Your sister tells me how to drive
—*Don't go too fast. Watch out for kids*—
as she hurtles past toward her shards of glass
and Appalachian dirt and grit,
forever freeze-framed in that flight,
Jeep in midair about to crash,
your bereft teenaged self
begging her not to leave.

Now we're past the bridge,
and melons from the Seward Co-op
are rolling on the floor.
The dudes from the Los Campeones gym,
each having bench-pressed
a single rhinoceros, flex
while sitting in chairs outside
watching the Saturday walkers.

We're counting on your fabled luck
even as it begins to drizzle.
Every green light blesses our momentum,
breakfasts from Maria's Café
soothing us with aromas
the way we need to be soothed—
just you and I now
trying to stay calm,

driving to emergency,
a slow car dawdling in front of us,
a short cut that's not a short cut,
windshield wipers and pedestrians
jangling our nerves, neither of us talking,
both lost in the tunnels of our thoughts.

Finally, an entrance in the rain
where ambulances slumber.

Breathing as best you can,
your stone weight presses down on me

as the doors open wide—

last moment in the world

before the hospital machinery
catches you in its gears.

ASH

Night in Havana
at the gangster's hotel
where the gold phone
presented to Batista
by the American ambassador
is still stashed away
in an office drawer,
the veranda open
to an ocean breeze.
Every day here
another building collapses
in the city center. Beauty
crumbling, then dying,
brings you back to me.
This afternoon along the Malecon
lovers perched on the seawall
with only the image
of the other in their eyes.
When I spilled your ashes,
some landing on rocks,
some on water,
I feared that, so divided,
you'd be lost. Finally,
a wave snatched you
like the hand of God,
and I watched a life dissolve,
waves receding
then indistinguishable.

WHY WE STILL WRITE POEMS AS THE COUNTRY SUCCUMBS TO MEANNESS

When I tire of a language of artifice
empty as a clapper without a bell,
I return to the flat speech of the Midwest,
to Georgia Hollrah's simple kindness
teaching English three nights a week
at Christ Lutheran, Dennison, Iowa,
each of her students with a story
worthy of a novel, crossing rivers
and borders to arrive at the idea
of America which starts here
where men with knuckles swollen from shifts
spent slashing out the guts of hogs,
and women whose eyes point down in shyness
or shame, struggle to wring some beauty
from strange guttural sounds, more like
the thunk of rain falling on cracked earth
than the vowels of their native Spanish.
The tenderness of September leaves outside
and the immense sky above the plains
holds them here in their adopted home,
while words won through faith and hard work
are passed on and on some more,
the way poetry begins with generosity.

A DREAM IN BLACK AND WHITE

Hiking up an alpine ridge
dressed in his brown suede coat—
no boots or crampons,
no ice ax or glasses for snow blindness
though the sheen is brilliant white—
you think of the house on Franklin,
an ordinary summer evening,
the garden hose hiss a serpent;
you, your brother in bathing suits,
laughing, receiving the spray,
cold surprise in the milky almost dark,
a boy's way of being hugged, and now
past the tree line you know you'll not descend again,
still, you climb easily, almost running,
as if growing lighter here,
as if floating on air.

THE HEART

But maybe the heart
doesn't want to be understood,
too busy stumbling through its hours
to accept the humility
of an old woman
wrestled from a wheelchair
and deposited in a church pew
by an attendant
who has wandered off to smoke a joint.

Just she and I now,
swimming this river of silence—
St. Janez, church of my grandmother
before she left for America—
this woman perhaps an ancient, distant aunt,
moving her mouth without sound,
her praying so much like simple breathing,
submitting to what is given,
like the leaves outside falling or about to fall.

Ljubljana, Slovenia

LAST LOOK

Last look,
scent of her sweat,
feet growing cold.
Last look,
hollow of years,
stream bed of tears
drying, dry,
face, body
to memorize.
Last look,
gathering keys,
pillow,
books, phone,
contact lens case,
insurance card,
plastic bag
filled with clothes
she wore
a week ago.
4062
of the ICU:
village of tubes,
octopus
of cords,
monitors,
lotions,
towels,
call button
fatigued.
Last look,
foot of the bed
she last

breathed in.
Last look,
turning,
turning away.

Last look

MY GARDEN NOW

The weekend before the snow falls,
I cover the plants with leaves,
rip out withered stalks
of the perennials thinking
of the time when nothing blooms.
Bending, I gather the crumpled leaves
strewn in their finality,
place them on the mound of dirt that tombs
the summer's roses. The sky,
terrifying and beautiful heaves downward
almost to the ground. And what is this wind
that blows through me as if I am an emptiness?
A garden hose slithers along the fence
draining drip by drip its down-turned mouth.

THIS MOMENT

Great stretches of time with our routines
ripped away from us.
And how I miss the movie theater's popcorn,
though now we're living a horror movie
no one knows the outcome of.

Yesterday, afraid, I walked in the woods
where a deer gazed for a full minute
as if she knew me. I wish I hadn't reached
for my camera,
but I thought it was you coming back to me.

I cried driving home, thinking of my losses
and losses yet to come. Then a car blazed on fire
at the edge of the freeway, no one in the car,
no one stopping—strange days—all of us
remembering to keep our distance away.

UNCOVERING THE ROSES

This world is not a home.

The phrase invades my mind
as I work kneeling and stretching
my arms out wide as I can manage
embracing the brittle leaves,
placing them in bags,

leaves that clothed the roses
through the winter's cold
and once sleeked the trees with color
when she was still alive.

                Bag after bag—
this world is not a home.
Kneel, stretch, release, repeat—
this patient attention
I deem numinous,
though she'd have refused the word.

I carry them down the stairs
three at a time,
balance walking the garden stones,
careful of the tulip shoots.

                Up above
in the street's skeletal canopy of limbs,
squirrels practice their acrobatics.
Through the spaces a spring sun finds me,
a lost and frightened child.

AUTUMN COMES TO THE NORTH SHORE

I step across boulders,
tree roots,
slick wet leaves,
going down into thick woods
the way my dead
must have traveled,
down to the cataract
of the waterfall
where white riffles
tumble over rocks
as chutes and runnels
carry the year away.
There I drop my pack—
body unclenching—
lean out into the spray,
wash my grief
in the cold stream.

THESE DAYS

These days I start out with nothing
but a blank page, the cough
of a truck outside switching gears,
a sad November sky, and matted leaves
on the ground of a city
whose memory of wildness,
asphalted and numbed over,
returns sometimes in dreams.
I drink my coffee, invoking the names
of the dead, then begin
to search the empty places,
picking up each rock
to gaze beneath where there is this
and this and that. *Pay attention,*
I tell myself, not sure
I know what I'm looking for.

IV

PILGRIMAGE, BLACKHAWK ISLAND

for Emily

The last hour of light of a January day,
father and daughter trudge through snow
to reach the poet's one-room cabin,

push open a door to the remains of a forge
where matter was transformed to spirit,
then condensed and condensed some more.

Long after the fact spirit fills the space.
They feel it, even see it rise to vapor
of a fog enshrouding the catalpa trees.

Nonetheless, it's easy to grasp a sense
of the poet's unvarnished sentiment:
walls thin as a writing tablet, no plumbing,

the river in all moods of weather,
a mercurial life companion,
one she'd never leave, the man thinks

as they turn back toward their footprints
and the icy ruts of the island road,
pleased to have found the place to show to her.

cabin of Lorine Niedecker,
Blackhawk Island, Wisconsin

ORDINARY TIME, JEFFERSON, IOWA

Let us praise the Hy-Vee store's breakfast buffet
and the town's people, churched, coffeed, satiated,
entirely without judgment, accepting it all like God
and swaying like comfortable bears as they eat.
Praise as well the absence of irony
as the town's carillon tower rises
twelve stories high, and for three dollars you'll ride
a lift to the top, then squint out the miles
flat as a monopoly board toward distant grain
elevators, east and west and north and south
looking exactly the same on this the twenty-fifth
Sunday of Ordinary Time, my joy now
in the ordinary well-scrubbed small-town streets,
the sparkling yellow coneflowers and butterflies,
even the blue and unfenced sky.

BICYCLING AS A FORM OF PRAYER

Lean a little forward on your seat.
Keep your rhythm, the same cadence,
no matter the climbs or dips.
Your tired muscles will revive.
Listen to wind murmur through a stand of trees.
See how leaves haloed in sun
shine greener than their usual hue.
Trimbelle Creek will hum the same lullaby
first heard when Cris was still alive.
Then though you know the route by heart,
the river rises up surprising and immense.
Receive it.
Receive the bluffs, their craggy old-man faces.
The hours are nothing. They will melt away.
Each mile joy will bring you closer to kindness
and then even closer still.

DIRT

Please Lord, help me
not look away
when those unlike myself
are hunted like beasts,

heard at a prayer service
here at George Floyd Square
almost a year ago. Chauvin guilty
now, yet already a half dozen
others shot, some in the back.

We each place the taproot
of a single crocus
maybe four inches into the earth
of the Say Their Names Cemetery.

A modest flower,
it accrues authority
by joining in numbers. Dirt
on our hands, we tamp down soil,
quietly kneeling, tamping.

BIRTHDAY

November 7th, 2020

Among the moving throng most were wearing masks.
Some pulled down their masks to breathe or weep

while a young man banged a drum, and cars passed honking horns—

something being born, a pressure finally released,
a beginning, beautiful in the way of beginnings, unblemished and uncertain,

oaks lifted from their roots, thick trunks twisting in a dance,
kites spiraled down at first then up, up searching the sky.

A woman, someone's grandmother, twirled around a pole,
singing, "Ding dong the witch is dead"—

everything reaching, lifting, soaring, dancing,
warm for November, the snow geese confused—

champagne, picnic basket, honey-roasted almonds,
strangers dancing with strangers.

"Easier now to tell your kids character matters," the man said on TV—
how the stranger who told me this began to cry,
and though there was a plague, I reached out to him.

ROSARY SOCIETY, ST. MARY'S CHURCH, RACINE, WISCONSIN

> *It's the soul that's erotic*
> —Adelia Prado

I see them at the nave of the church
alone in the pews after Mass—
the priest gone,
the children shepherded back to school—
their call and response over and again
reciting prayers known by heart.

I say I see them though the verb is wrong,
for they have reached an age
where they are invisible,
no longer gazed at by the world
though beautiful now
the way winter trees are beautiful.

Hail Mary full of grace,
the Lord is with thee—
their bodies grained in smoky light,
they stay entranced
the better part of the morning,
making slow love to their Christ.

POEM FOR THE DOG JAYA

Generous teacher,
I begin to fathom
what you've tried to convey

about enthusiasm,
how it opens each moment
to an ordinary radiance,

how the wind speaks
the language of trees,
though it's much easier for you,

living in a world without names
or only a single name,
which is *world*,

every new face
divine enough
to deserve your love.

19 WADHAM GARDENS

for Elizabeth

As if thirty years hadn't passed,
everything in its place,
a row of prim Edwardians,
hedges neatly trimmed,
your house the second from the last,
next door to the Tory MP
who once made a pass at you;

the spacious front room with its sea of glass,
your roses changing color and hue
with each angle of light
and the long hallway,
its vestibule an estuary
flowing to a harbor of kitchen smells
and scenes of family life;

a young American mother and wife
in love
with the vista stretched before you,
when things made sense,
even the English weather.
There it is, you point,
trying to pull me into that dream.

Now it's raining or almost raining
or about to clear into sun.
We walk the blocks to Primrose Hill,
you, turning back only once.
Sweetie, I know there's no logic to it,
how it is
we've been allowed a second life.

DAYS OF BEES AND INDIGO

In those days of bees and indigo,
        those days of blue delphinium,
I passed the peonies without a glance
        to bend to the scent
                of a row of roses.

Lili was a sparrow then,
        an apprentice mimicking
the way I matched the peacock
        we had watched,
backside thrust in air, strutting

and equally my sniffing
        just so
and equally her body bent
        parallel to the ground,
those days of summer

that have passed
        like windows closing.
                And so, write them
in the book, the names, the mysteries,
        we owe them at least that.

WHAT TO DO IN NEW YORK CITY

Walk. Walk along a flow of beings
to a confluence of other beings.
Walk the broad avenues
whose monolithic towers scaffold skyward
like stacked money ascending to God.
Notice faces along the sidewalk
pressed against the warmth of buildings,
laying or sitting,
their possessions carried in a bag.
Walk past the leashed poodles,
doodles, and kidney-shaped Chihuahuas.
Walk without a plan on side streets, dark but vibrant.
Squeeze between the jostling crowds.
Watch for traffic. Consult your maps.
Smell odors unapologetically human.
Descend subterranean subway caves
or climb up to the Highline, walking, walking.

It's true you've lived many lives.
Live this one now, walking it
past windows opening to other lives.
Imagine them but desire only this.
Stop for a beer. Observe the river
yawning and stretching.
Listen to the languages around you.
Now resume walking.
Don't ask where you're going.
Let darkness fold around you
as rain disperses equally
on the self-possessed and the dispossessed.
For the time being it is summer.
For the time being you are no one,
only the breeze, the rain, and the weeds

sprouting between cracks of asphalt.
Don't ask how much time is left.
Just walk.

THIS

This green day, each purified breath,
    this coffee
and the morning's deep distress,
    inexplicably soothed
by watching trains slumber in their yard
and the brakeman slowly inspect
each coupling, hose and coil.

One day closer to the time I will be nothing,
    even in someone's memory,
I receive the peace of this peaceful sign:
    ALL ARE WELCOME HERE
these morning walkers, these bikers,
this thwack of a tennis racquet
against a rocket-launched-like ball,
the soft right ear of this grateful dog
    nosing up to greet me,
this white sleeve of its owner's blouse,
    this green, this yellow, this red.

I thank my life for the love I hold,
    misplace
then retrieve again and again,
    thank it
for my childhood wounds
that awakened and blessed me,
thank this torch of purple lilacs,
    the new grass,
and the birdsongs that have returned.

OCTOBER JOURNAL

OCTOBER 8

From this day I take the image
of the golden eagles
circling above the Kinnickinnic River.
I take the sound of moving water
and the progress of a maple leaf
tumbling over pebbles in the stream.
I take the fly fisherman
practicing his art,
take the minutes we were lost,
finding our way back to the car.

Most of all I take the two-year-old black Lab
who shyly allowed me to pet her.
"When we first got her," the owner said,
"she had been so cruelly treated,
all her foot pads were torn off."

I take her joy diving in a pile of leaves,
guileless creature, who learned to trust again.

OCTOBER 9

We eat tacos for Joel's birthday.
I carry to the diner
the cadence of a bicycle ride,
breath synced with the pedaling,
orange-gold leaves reflected on the water.

October 11

How could the mechanic lock my keys
inside the car?
My anger was a rising force
that I managed to keep down.

With a shim and a metal snake
in twenty minutes, the job was done,
and I was free,
righteous, and spent to drive home.

What was so precious about my time
that I couldn't abide that harmless farce?

October 12 (Lake of the Isles, 7 a.m.)

No one on the usually busy trail.
Gradually my eyes discern a line of ducks
swimming in a row.

Do I see trees walking along shore?
I hallucinate a stick
navigating by itself.

Out of the shadows,
the blind man Mahesh appears,
accompanied by his dog, Vino.

October 15

First hard frost—
the elephant-eared plant flaps
in a stiff north breeze.

A change of weather,
leaves scattered or scattering,
a shabby, humbled radiance in the trees,
thinned out but holding on.

No more easy, light-infused morning walks.
No more suppers on the deck.

October 19

Who was that man with my name
who lived with that wife, that daughter, in that house?
I walk out into the dark,
dawn's meager light illuminating snow
crusted on leaves, clinging to branches,
still more matted in clumps
on lawns and driveways.

I imagine bodies in Ukraine
piled in open graves.
Fear foreshadows something moving toward me.
Maybe I've turned on the car radio,
maybe the heater.
Another day begins
in my tenure on this earth,
but I'm not there.

October 21

As summer has returned
why not take the scenic route around the lake?
Why not change into your tennis shoes?
Why not stop to pet the passing dogs?

As summer has returned
why not try a little humor
with the stony-faced employee
at Department of Vehicle Services.

"Can you make it look like I have hair,"
I ask about the license photograph.
She orders me back in line,
says I closed my eyes though I know I didn't.

October 24

No rain in over a month.
Wind leaves a coat of dust on cars.
A twelve-foot-high skeleton
looms in front of my neighbor's house.

November 1

"When we disconnect the breathing tube,"
we told Cris,
"your organs will shut down.
We won't do it unless you're ready."

"Rest," she whispered.
Hours later we brought it up again.
Yes, she nodded.
I still marvel at that bravery.

We each held one of her hands,
traveling with her as far as we could.

Now she's an accomplished soul,
and I love another woman.
On this day when the two worlds come so near
I almost touch her hand again.

NOTES ON THE POEMS

Solitudes, III: The italicized material is from Amos 5:11

Why We Still Write Poems as the Country Succumbs to Meanness: This poem was inspired by the fine book *Dennison, Iowa: Searching for the Soul of America Through the Secrets of a Midwest Town* by Dale Maharidge which explores how small-town America is being changed by immigration

Birthday: November 7th was the day Joe Biden was declared the winner of the 2020 election. It was also my 67th birthday.

The poem "October Journal" owes a debt to Thomas R. Smith's book *Medicine Year*.

TITLE INDEX

Numbers
19 Wadham Gardens 75

A
A Dream in Black and White 57
Advent 47
A Free Man 20
An Accounting 46
Ash 55
Autumn Comes to
   the North Shore 64

B
Beer 28
Bicycling as a Form of Prayer 70
Birthday 72

C
Cass Lake 37
Copycat Music 23
Crazy Love 34

D

Days of Bees and Indigo 76
Dirt 71
Downtown Minneapolis 38

E

East of the Cheyenne Reservation 49
Election Day, November 2016 30
Elysium 26

F

First Death 19
First Session 48
First Summer of the Trump Presidency 32

G

Gardener 15

H

Here 39

K

Kickapoo, Most Crooked of Rivers 31

L

Last Look 59

M

My Garden Now 61

N

New York City Poem for Emily 27

O

October Journal 80
Ordinary Time, Jefferson, Iowa 69

P

Paper Route 21
Pilgrimage, Blackhawk Island 68
Poem for the Dog Jaya 74
Praise Song for Feet 16
Proletarian Poet 45

R

Rosary Society, St. Mary's Church, Racine, Wisconsin 73

S

Solitudes 40
South Side 18

T

The Dancers 44
The Heart 58
The Parlor 50
These Days 65
The Wrestlers 35
This 79
This Is It 52
This Moment 62

U

Uncovering the Roses 63

W

What To Do in New York City 77
When I Was a King 14
Why We Still Write Poems as the
    Country Succumbs to Meanness 56
Wisconsin Supper Club 25

FIRST LINE INDEX

A

Among the moving throng most were wearing masks 72
And after the rain there was bird song and we drove 26
And for your crimes against humanity, Mr. Trump 46
As a Hunter's moon stalks the streets of old northeast 34
As August light slanted golden on the leaves 27
As if thirty years hadn't passed 75
At an early '90s memorial for Thomas McGrath 45
At the doorway introduction 48

B

Because I was a king 14
But maybe the heart 58

E

Eva dying in the apartment facing the alley 18

F

From this day I take the image 80

G

Generous teacher 74
Great stretches of time with our routines 62

H

Here the invisible gremlins which
  hover around us have swooped 39
Hiking up an alpine ridge 57

I

In Amsterdam a poet is hired to attend the funerals 40
I never asked his name 23
In those days of bees and indigo 76
In those days when there was no king 47
I see them at the nave of the church 73
I step across boulders 64
I watch her on her knees 15

L

Last look 59
Lean a little forward on your seat 70
Let us praise the Hy-Vee store's breakfast buffet 69

N

Night in Havana 55

O

One who goes here and then there 31

P

Please Lord, help me 71

S

Some of us still snuggle 16
Something askew in the universe now 32
Some winter days the sheen off the lake can be blinding ... 37
Summer, the college town half full, maybe less 20

T

The last hour of light of a January day 68
The locals share a body type 25
The not so ironically surnamed 19
The poem asks 44
There where the Missouri surges 49
These days I start out with nothing 65
The weekend before the snow falls 61
They come to this parlor of alchemy 50
This green day, each purified breath 79
This world is not a home 63
Three days after we buried her 30
Today I wrestled the devil anxiety 35

W

Walking up and down stairs 21
Walk. Walk along a flow of beings 77
Whatever is going to happen has already happened 38
When I tire of a language of artifice 56
Who knows where my father 28

Y

You bring *The New York Times* with you 52